DRIED FLOWERS
A Handbook: A to Z

DRIED FLOWERS
A Handbook: A to Z

Sue Nicholls

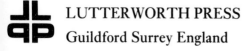 LUTTERWORTH PRESS
Guildford Surrey England

First published 1984

ISBN 0-7188-2590-X

Set in Ehrhardt 10/10½ by
Butler & Tanner Ltd, Frome and London
Printed in Great Britain by
Butler & Tanner Ltd, Frome and London

Contents

Acknowledgements

I would like to thank Bill Denny, Head of Malvern College
Art Department, and Peter Scott, one of his students;
Heritage Portraits of Malvern; and my friends and family
who have given me help and encouragement.

Sue Nicholls

Colour Plates

Plates 1, 2 and 3, taken by Heritage Portraits
of Malvern, appear between pages 32 and 33.
Each is faced by a key drawing identifying
the dried flowers and foliage shown in the
plate. An alphabetical list of the plants
shown appears on page 62.

TO
MY MOTHER

Introduction

This hand-book is written for gardeners and flower lovers as a simple guide to drying flowers and it has been made as comprehensible as possible.

Even people who have no garden from which to pick can gather material from hedgerows, window boxes, pot plants and so on.

Not many years ago 'dried flowers' used to conjure up a picture of dreary, dusty, brown flowers stuck in a vase in the corner of a room. Not so today. If flowers are picked at the right time and dried properly in a dark, warm, airy place, they can look almost as lovely as any fresh arrangement.

The secret of success is in the time of picking. If a flower is picked at its most beautiful, preferably when the sap is rising in the middle of the day and when the weather is fine, and then dried, it will give summer colour in a home throughout the winter. If you have to pick a flower after rain, shake it gently and then put it in water, and wait until all the moisture has disappeared from the petals before preserving.

The glossary covers a great many garden flowers and shrubs that dry well; there are sure to be others, which can be discovered only by experiment and patience. There is also a supplementary list (pages 55-9) suggesting some wild flowers, foliage, etc., which dry successfully.

Drying by Hanging and Drying Upright

Some flowers need to be dried in a greater heat than others; some need no heat at all. The perfect place would be a well-ventilated, warm, dark room, such as an attic or cellar where there is a hot tank. A linen cupboard, too, is very good, especially for flowers needing quick drying. A corner of a spare room can be used as long as it is airy and away from strong sunlight, and even a shed or summerhouse, if quite dry and well ventilated, is perfectly all right for some flowers, such as yarrow or golden rod, that do not need heat. But there is no doubt that most flowers keep their colour best when dried in a warm, airy place, and in the dark.

It is always better to hang large flowers separately (e.g., delphinium, peony, dahlia, etc.) so that they do not touch each other; but most may be hung in bunches. These are better bound in elastic bands since the stems shrink as they dry. Alternatively, tie them with raffia or gardener's twine, but make sure to tighten this as the flowers dry.

It is not possible to be specific about the length of time needed to dry the flowers, but in general they are ready when they feel dry and crisp to the touch and the stems are firm. Make sure that the stems are dry right to the top, near the flower, which is usually the last place to dry out. If they are not, the flowers drop when they are stored.

Once the drying is complete, be sure to store the flowers or leaves in a dry place. If left in a damp or humid atmosphere they will soon go limp.

Quite a number of flowers (e.g., spiraea or astilbe) dry just as well, or better, upright in a container, such as a jam jar or a large vase, according to the size of the material to be preserved. But most still need a warm, ventilated atmosphere. The chief reason for upright drying is that it preserves the shape of the stem or flowerhead better than if they were hung. Flowers requiring upright drying will be indicated under their separate headings.

Delicate grasses are better dried flat. They then retain their natural shapes and the stems are less likely to break.

Preserving in Glycerine

This treatment is very good for preserving sprays or small branches of trees and shrubs. They will keep their shape but their foliage turns varying colours. Mature stems preserve better than young growth, so most gathering can be left till mid to late summer while the tree or shrub is still taking up moisture. But once the leaves have started to turn colour, they will not glycerine well.

The solution is made up by mixing two parts of hot water to one part of glycerine (this can be bought from most chemists' shops). Alternatively, anti-freeze liquid can be used, mixing one part of anti-freeze to one part of hot water (or, if the stems are very woody, boiling water). Mix very thoroughly before use. Glycerine is preferable and more successful as the anti-freeze, though cheaper, is inclined to turn some sprays an unnatural colour. Only the first few inches of the stems need be covered, so a narrow container is advisable. This can in turn be placed in a larger and heavier receptacle to hold the weight of the stems. Be sure to preserve only perfect specimens, removing any damaged leaves first. Split the end of each stem and stand in warm water for a few hours before transferring to the glycerine solution. Discard any stems that may have wilted in the meantime. If the liquid is absorbed before preservation is complete, top it up to the original level with more of the solution. An indication that the treatment is complete is when the leaves turn colour. If moisture comes out of the pores of the leaves, remove at once, wipe off any surplus with a cloth and hang in a dry room. If the stems are left in the solution too long and are not really dry when stored, a mould is liable to form.

Some large and very leathery leaves, which might otherwise take a long time to absorb the solution, are best sponged with, or even immersed in, the glycerine before treatment, e.g. *Fatsia japonica* and *Aspidistra*.

After it has been used the solution can be stored in an airtight bottle or container and used again. But it should be boiled before doing so.

If a lighter colour is required, preserve as described and then stand the sprays or stems in a sunny window.

Many types of foliage can be preserved in this way. Some are mentioned specifically in the Glossary and in the supplementary list (pages 55–8), but others that are not included are *Aucuba japonica* (Spotted Laurel), *Garrya elliptica* and *Prunus laurocerasus* (Common Laurel); also camellia, oleaster (*Eleagnus*), magnolia, mahonia, oak and rhododendron.

All these need to be treated for about three or four weeks.

Drying by Pressing

A large range of leaves and sprays can be dried by this method, some drying better than others. It is advisable to pick the material when it is mature and dry. For instance, the new young growth of fern picked in May does not press as well as fern picked in June or later.

Leaves and sprays can be pressed between sheets of newspaper or brown paper under a carpet, a mattress or a sofa cushion, or between blotting-paper in a book, according to size. A warning note should be sounded, however, over the use of newspaper as the print is inclined to come off on some leaves, though this does not appear to happen with ferns. Care must be taken to see that the leaves or sprays are pressed in their natural curves; the individual leaves of a spray must not be twisted, and the fronds of ferns should be lying correctly.

Leave them to dry for about six weeks, after which they can be stored for future use.

Some leaves can be pressed between sheets of brown paper or blotting-paper with a warm iron. This is much quicker, but the result is not as satisfactory and the process produces a rather unpleasant smell.

Among the most useful leaves to dry for natural arrangements are acanthus, bamboo, dogwood (*Cornus*), hellebore, montbretia, and peony. Maidenhair fern (*Adiantum*) is also very valuable, as are other ferns.

Drying by Desiccants

If you have the time and patience to dry flowers by this method, it is very rewarding.

The simplest desiccant to use is silica gel, though it is expensive. It can be obtained from most chemists' shops and comes in the form of small white crystals which should be ground down before use. I use a liquidiser, making sure to keep the lid on as a cloud of fine white dust will billow up.

Household borax can also be used. It is cheaper than silica gel and can be bought from any hardware shop. It is inclined to become lumpy when damp, but the lumps can easily be broken up or put through a sieve once the borax has been dried. In fact, it is advisable to run *any* desiccant through a sieve from time to time to remove any small unwanted particles.

Sand has been used as a desiccant for very many years, but it is not nearly as satisfactory as the other two. Firstly, it needs a great deal of preparation: it has to be washed and dried thoroughly, and all extraneous 'bodies' must be removed, until it is smooth and runs easily through the fingers. And it does not dry flowers nearly as fast as the other desiccants.

Make sure that the dessicant is completely dry before use. A humidity indicator (supplied with each packet of silica gel) is a great help, as it will show whether the desiccant is dry or damp. In the latter case, spread the desiccant on a baking tray and leave it in a cool oven for about twenty minutes to dry out.

When choosing the flowers, be careful to pick perfect specimens and remove all blemished and unwanted leaves. To dry them you need a flat container or box. Some people say an airtight lid is required, but I have dried vast quantities of flowers without one and they have been very satisfactory. Cover the base of the container with desiccant and then put in the flower, arranging it to lie in its natural shape. Some can be laid flat, others face down or face up, according to the shape of the flower. Then work the desiccant into all corners of the flower with your fingers or a brush so that every part is covered. No two flowers should touch. It is advisable not to dry too many flowers at once, especially if you are mixing flowers of different kinds, as they will require varying times, some longer, some shorter, to dry out. It is a good idea to put the container in a warm room or on top of a radiator, or even in the linen cupboard, as it dries the flowers out quicker and keeps the desiccant dry. The length of time required for drying varies according to the texture of the flower and stem. Naturally, the thicker the stem the longer it will take to dry out. Before removing all the flowers test one by gently placing your fingers below the flower and lifting it out. If it is not completely dry it can be put back for a little longer.

Some flowers appear to have dried beautifully, but after a few weeks they go limp and lose their beauty. This is often because they have been introduced into a damp atmosphere, so it is important to store them somewhere really dry. Most flowers change their colour very slightly, some going a little darker and others more muted. Yellow, orange and blue flowers seem to hold their colour best.

Rough estimates of the length of time needed for drying by desiccant are indicated in the Glossary, under the individual entries, but there are many other flowers besides those described there that would react favourably to this treatment. A few are mentioned below:

Anemone	4 days
Camellia	6 days
Chionodoxa	2 to 3 days
Cyclamen	2 days
Daffodils (small trumpet variety)	4 days
Hyacinth (wire stem)	4 days
Pansy	3 days
Primrose	2 days
Pulmonaria	3 days
Snowdrop	2 to 3 days
Violet	2 days
Wallflower	3 to 4 days

Arranging

I do not pretend to be an expert flower arranger, but perhaps a few tips may not go amiss.

Of course, as in fresh flower arranging, the 'mechanics' are all-essential: that is, choosing the right size and shape of container, and preparing it with dry foam, or chicken-wire (the two-inch size), or a pinholder. Personally, I find foam good for small dried arrangements, as long as it is very firmly based, and chicken-wire surrounding foam for larger arrangements. If the 'mechanics' are not perfect, then neither will the arrangement be.

In most arrangements you will need more dried flowers than would be the case if you were using fresh flowers. With smaller flowers (e.g., lavender, love-in-a-mist, rhodanthe, xeranthemum), it is better to bunch them, or at least to group several stems together, as this gives more colour than would a single individual flower. As dried flowers are more delicate than fresh ones, it is a good idea first to cover your base with moss or 'filler' flowers (e.g., hydrangea heads, chamomile or catmint) which in addition will give bulk to the centre of the arrangement and help to hold other delicate stems in position. The arrangement can then be built up around this.

Short bunches of flowers can be lengthened with the use of florist's wires, and an individual flower can either be lengthened in the same way or by inserting its stem into the discarded hollow stem of some larger flower.

There are lists on pages 59-61 to help the less-experienced flower gatherer with colour combinations.

Glossary

GARDEN FLOWERS AND SHRUBS FOR DRYING

ACANTHUS
BEAR'S BREECHES   Perennial

Hooded white and light purple flowers borne on spikes 3 to 4 feet high (90 to 120 cm) in July to August. Pick when fully in flower—or as near as possible—and hang in a warm room. Alternatively, allow to dry off in water, which should not be topped up. These are dramatic flowers for a large floral arrangement. The leaves press well.

ACHILLEA
YARROW   Perennial

Gold, pale yellow or carmine flat-headed flowers growing on stiff stems 3 to 4 feet tall (90 to 120 cm) from June to September. The leaves are fern-like. 'Coronation Gold' is a strong yellow, while 'Flowers of Sulphur' or 'Moonshine' are softer and prettier. 'Fire King' is carmine. Do not pick until the tiny florets have formed hard centres—if picked too soon the head will divide—and then hang individually so that they will not cut into other heads and spoil their shape. Alternatively, they can be picked earlier and put in a little

ACANTHUS:
BEAR'S BREECHES

13

warm water to dry off, but do not top up the water. The carmine flowers turn pale as the stamens harden.

A. ptarmica (Sneezewort), of which 'Pearl' and 'Perry's White' are good varieties, has clusters of little, double, white, button-like flowers on stems 2 to 3 feet tall (60 to 90 cm) from June to August. The leaves are narrow and lanceolate. Pick when in full flower, but not turning brown, and hang.

ACROCLINIUM syn. HELIPTERUM
—*A. Roseum* Annual

Double or semi-double, pink or white, daisy-like flowers with yellow or dark centres, on stems 1 to $1\frac{1}{2}$ feet high (30 to 45 cm), flowering June to August. Either sow out of doors in April to May, where they are to flower, or—preferably—sow under glass in March and plant out when large enough to handle, to flower six weeks later. Pick when flowers are just opening and hang in bunches. A very valuable addition to any arrangement. See also *RHODANTHE.*

AFRICAN LILY, see *AGAPANTHUS*

AGAPANTHUS—*A. africanus*
AFRICAN LILY Perennial

Blue or white funnel-shaped flowers borne in umbels on erect stems 2 to $2\frac{1}{2}$ feet tall (60 to 75 cm) in late summer. Pick seedheads when pods have swollen but are still green, and hang. They turn an attractive gold colour and form a good shape in a large arrangement.

AGERATUM
FLOSS FLOWER Annual

Fluffy-headed clusters of blue, lilac, pink or

ACROCLINIUM

14

white flowers used for edging borders. It is not worth growing these specifically for drying. They flower from May to the first frost. Pick when just out and hang to dry. Use them in small arrangements, or at the base of large ones as 'filler'.

ALCHEMILLA—A. mollis
LADY'S MANTLE   Perennial

Clumps of pale green, palmate leaves with fluffy sprays of yellow calyces on stems 18 inches tall (45 cm) in June to August. Cut when fully out but before the tiny flowers turn brown. Remove the larger leaves and either hang or dry upright. The leaves can also be pressed. Alchemilla responds well to glycerine treatment and turns a golden brown colour.

ALLIUM

There are a number of ornamental species, among which are *A. Rosenbachianum* with large purple-lilac heads, *A. roseum* with small purple flowers and *A. Moly* with bright yellow star-shaped flowers, all good for drying. Pick when the flowers have opened, and hang or dry upright.

See also LEEKS, in the next section.

ALTHAEA—A. rosea
HOLLYHOCK   Annual, biennial, perennial

Single or double, trumpet-shaped flowers in shades of crimson, rose, white and yellow, on spikes 6 to 8 feet tall (2 to 3 metres) in July and August. The leaves are lobed and rough. Pick the spikes at the length you require, when the seedheads have formed but are still green. Remove the leaves and hang. They turn an attractive pale green and are useful for their height and the bold outline that they give to a large arrangement.

AMARANTHUS:
LOVE-LIES-BLEEDING:
see page 16

15

AMARANTHUS—*A. caudatus*
LOVE-LIES-BLEEDING   Annual

Half-hardy annual, with crimson drooping tassels flowering July to October, growing on stems 3 to 4 feet tall (90 to 120 cm) with ovate leaves. Sow seeds under glass in March and plant out in May, or alternatively sow straight into the ground in a sunny position in April. Pick as soon as the tassels are red, remove the leaves and dry upright in a container in a little water, which should not be topped up.

There is also a *Viridis* variety with green tassels, known as Love-in-Idleness, which dries equally well.

For an illustration, see page 15.

AMMOBIUM—*A. alatum*
SAND FLOWER   Annual

Half-hardy, with a yellow-centred flower sur-rounded by white bracts. Sow under glass in March and plant out in May. The seeds are not easy to get and usually have to be specially ordered, but are worth it as this is a very useful addition to any dried arrangement. Pick when the flowers are just beginning to open; if left until fully open, the centre turns dark and is not nearly as attractive. Hang in bunches. The plants will survive for a second year if the frosts are not too severe.

ANAPHALIS
PEARL EVERLASTING   Perennial

Grey-foliage plants with clusters of small off-white flowers appearing in late summer. Pick when the flowers are just open and hang. If picked too late the flowers will become fluffy and drop. Remove any dark or damaged leaves.

For an illustration, see the facing page.

AMMOBIUM

ANTHEMIS—*A. nobilis*
CHAMOMILE

This plant, which has white, daisy-like flowers borne on spraying stems in May to September, with aromatic green foliage, is often found growing wild on waste ground and at waysides. Pick when fully in flower, strip the leaves and hang in bunches. This is very useful as 'filler' in dried arrangements.

Chamomile does not entirely lose its smell on drying and it is often used as an insecticide.

AQUILEGIA
COLUMBINE   Perennial

Funnel-shaped flowers with spurs in shades of pink, purple, blue, yellow, crimson and white, growing on stems $1\frac{1}{2}$ to 2 feet high (45 to 60 cm) in early summer. The flowers do not dry but the seedheads make lovely shapes. Pick when the petals have fallen and the seedheads are well formed, still green, and beginning to turn outwards. Either dry upright or hang.

ARBUTUS—A. Unedo
STRAWBERRY TREE

Dark green, ovate, leathery leaves with urn-shaped, pinkish-white flowers in October to November, forming clusters of strawberry-like fruits. Pick mature sprays and treat in glycerine for about four to six weeks. The leaves will retain their green colour but turn a little darker.

ARTEMISIA   Perennial

There are numerous species of this plant, mostly grown for their silvery-grey foliage, and they all dry well. Pick when mature, but before the weather has spoiled the leaves;

ANAPHALIS:
PEARL EVERLASTING:
see facing page

17

either hang, or dry upright in a container holding a little water which should not be topped up.

ARUNCUS—A. sylvester
GOAT'S BEARD   Perennial

Formerly included in the genus *Spiraea* as *S. Aruncus*, this shrub has creamy-white plumes growing on strong stems 4 to 6 feet long (120 to 180 cm), with light green, lanceolate leaves. Pick when first fully in bloom before the plumes begin to turn brown. Remove most of the leaves. Dry upright in containers with no water.

ASTER   Annual

Only the small double asters dry. They keep their colour well but turn a little darker. Sow in March or April under glass, prick out when seedlings are large enough and plant out in late May or early June for flowering in August and September. Pick when fully out and hang in a good heat. Although the petals may feel dry, check that the base of the flower just above the stem is also dry, otherwise it will disintegrate.

ASTILBE   Perennial

Crimson, pink, lilac or white plumes on stems 1 to 2 feet tall (30 to 60 cm) with feathery leaves, grown best in shade in a moist position. Pick when fully out, or as near to it as possible, and dry upright in a container with no water. These dry very quickly and are a very good and delicate addition to any arrangement. The feathery leaves can also be dried naturally, or individually pressed.

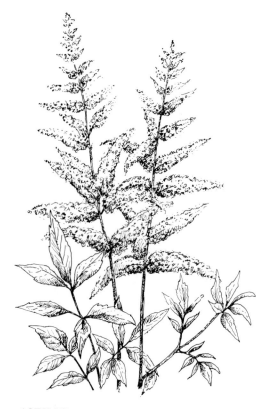

ASTILBE

18

ASTRANTIA
MASTERWORT

Perennial

Pink or white flowers with papery bracts and tripartite toothed leaves, on stems 1 to 2 feet tall (30 to 60 cm) in June or July. They dry very easily if picked when fully open. Strip the leaves and either hang or dry upright.

The seedheads are also very attractive and dry naturally on their stems.

BALLOTA

Perennial

Low-growing, much-branched shrub with heart-shaped, woolly, grey leaves. Whorls, in which tiny white flowers spotted with purple appear in July, encircle the stem. Do not pick until the flowers appear. Then strip the leaves, only the whorls remaining, and hang in bunches.

For an illustration, see overleaf.

BAMBOO, see next section

BAY, see next section

BEAR'S BREECHES, see *ACANTHUS*

BEECH, see next section

BELLS OF IRELAND, see *MOLUC-CELLA*

BERGENIA
syn. *MEGASEA*
ELEPHANT'S EAR

Perennial

Large, green, round or oval-shaped, leathery leaves which sometimes turn crimson in autumn. Heads of rose-purple, bell-shaped

ASTRANTIA:
MASTERWORT

19

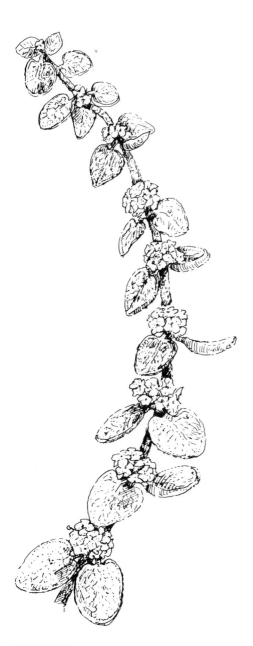

flowers appear on stems 12 inches tall (30 cm) in January to April each year. Pick the flowers when mature and hang in a good heat. The quicker they are dried the better they will retain their colour, but the stems take a long time to dry out.

For an illustration, see facing page.

BLANKET FLOWER, see *GAILLARDIA*

BLAZING STAR, see *LIATRIS*

BLUEBELL, see *SCILLA*

BOCCONIA—B. microcarpa
syn. Macleaya microcarpa
PLUME POPPY   Perennial

Bronze-coloured flowers borne in feathery panicles on stems 6 to 8 feet tall (2 to 3 metres) from June to August. The leaves are large and veined. *M. Cordata* has white plumes. Pick the stems once the flowers are over, and dry upright. They make a very graceful outline at the back of large arrangements.

BOX, see next section

BROOM, see *CYTISUS*

BUDDLEIA
BUTTERFLY BUSH

There are many species of this large, branching, deciduous or evergreen shrub with long, conical-shaped flowers—purple, white, pink or lavender—appearing from June to September. They all dry well, though the white species does not keep a good colour when

BALLOTA:
see page 19

20

dried. Pick when fully in flower, or as near to it as possible, before any of the tiny florets die. Strip the leaves and hang.

BURNING BUSH, see *KOCHIA*

BUTTERFLY BUSH, see *BUDDLEIA*

CALENDULA—C. officinalis
POT MARIGOLD   Annual

Single or double, orange or yellow, daisy-like flowers on stems 1 to 2 feet tall (30 to 60 cm), from May to the first frosts. The leaves are light green and lance-shaped, and have a pungent smell. Sow in a sunny position from March to April, or in September for early flowering the following year. They seed readily. Only the double varieties dry well. Pick when the flower first opens; either hang in a very warm atmosphere, such as a linen cupboard, or dry for half an hour in the oven (Regulo $\frac{1}{4}$ or 200°) or dry in desiccants for three or four days.

CAPE GOOSEBERRY, see *PHYSALIS*

CARNATION, see *DIANTHUS*

CARROT, see next section

CARYOPTERIS

Deciduous shrub up to 3 feet high (about 1 metre) with lavender-blue flowers appearing in clusters along the stems in August and September. It has small grey-green leaves. Either cut when all the flowers are as nearly out as possible and hang to dry in bunches, or

BERGENIA:
ELEPHANT'S EAR:
see page 19

21

leave until the seedheads have formed naturally and then gather.

CATANANCHE—*C. caerulea*
CUPID'S DART   Perennial

Electric-blue, semi-double, daisy-like flowers with papery bracts on stems 2 to 3 feet tall (60 to 90 cm), with narrow leaves, flowering late June to September. These do not dry satisfactorily by hanging, but if they are dried in desiccants for two or three days, they will keep their colour well.

For an illustration, see facing page.

CATMINT, see *NEPETA*

CEANOTHUS

There are two main groups of this shrub, bearing clusters of blue or mauve-blue flowers.

The evergreen varieties, very often trained against walls, flower in May and June, and the deciduous ones, which grow in loosely shaped branches, flower in summer and in the early autumn.

Cut when the flowers are fully out before they start fading or falling, and hang. With the evergreen varieties, gather whole sprays to add both green and hazy blue to an arrangement; with the deciduous variety—especially 'Gloire de Versailles'—it is better to pick single shoots, allowing further shoots to mature along the stem.

CELOSIA—*C. argentea plumosa*
Annual

Plumes of crimson, orange and yellow on stems 1 to 3 feet (30 to 90 cm) with narrow, almost stalkless, leaves. Sow in pots under

CARYOPTERIS:
see page 21

22

glass in March and leave to grow on steadily. They can be planted out in mid-June. Pick when just fully out, remove the leaves and hang to dry.

For an illustration, see overleaf.

CENTAUREA—C. Cyanus Annual
CORNFLOWER, KNAPWEED

Flowers of the traditional blue, but also of mauve, pink, crimson and white, on stems 2 to 3 feet tall (60 to 90 cm), with long, narrow leaves. Sow in a sunny bed in March to April and thin out. Pick when first fully open, bunch and dry very quickly, in good heat, such as a linen cupboard, or for half an hour in a low oven, at Regular $\frac{1}{4}$ or 200°.

CHAMOMILE, see *ANTHEMIS*

CHINESE LANTERN, see *PHYSALIS*

CHIVES, see next section

CHOISYA—C. ternata
MEXICAN ORANGE

Evergreen shrub 4 to 6 feet high ($1\frac{1}{4}$ to $1\frac{3}{4}$ metres) with shiny green leaves and clusters of white scented flowers, blooming from May onwards.

The flowers will dry in desiccants although their white will eventually fade.

Whole stems of choisya dry well in glycerine and will turn a lovely parchment colour. Keep them in the solution until the leaves have absorbed it fully.

For an illustration, see page 25.

CHRISTMAS ROSE, see *HELLEBORUS*

CATANANCHE:
CUPID'S DART:
see facing page

23

CHRYSANTHEMUM   Perennial

Though this is a large family, only a few varieties dry. Of the *C. Maximum* (Shasta Daisy) type, only 'Wirral Supreme', which has double white, daisy-like flowers in July, and dark green, lanceolate, toothed leaves, dries well.

The small pompom chrysanthemums, such as 'Cameo', also dry well, as does *C. Parthenium* (Feverfew). Some varieties of the latter, e.g. 'Snow Dwarf' and 'Gold Star', have white or yellow daisy-like flowers on stems 9 to 18 inches tall (20 to 40 cm) in July to September, and aromatic, light green leaves, and can be grown from seed.

Pick when the flowers are fully out, remove leaves and hang.

CLARKIA   Annual

White, pink or purple, single or double flowers on thin spikes 2 to $2\frac{1}{2}$ feet tall (60 to 75 cm). Sow in a sunny position in March or April. Pick when as many flowers on the stem as possible are fully out and hang or dry upright. They keep their colour well.

CLARY, see *SALVIA*

CLEMATIS

Deciduous or evergreen climbers up to 20 or 30 feet high (6 to 9 metres), bearing flowers which vary in size from small to large, and colour over a vast range, from March to October. The seedheads of almost all of them can be dried and will be useful in either large or small arrangements. Pick when hairy but not fluffy. If they are then hung to dry, a few

CELOSIA:
see page 23

24

heads in each bunch, they will become fluffy and will require no further treatment. They only fall if left too long before picking. Some heads form yellow balls, e.g. 'Nellie Moser' and 'Mrs Cholmondeley', and others grey, e.g. *C. macropetala*.

COLUMBINE, see *AQUILEGIA*

CONVALLARIA
LILY OF THE VALLEY   Perennial

Sweet-smelling sprays of white bells on stems about 12 inches tall (30 cm) in spring. Dry in desiccants for one day. They remain white for a while but then turn cream. The leaves do not press well.

CORNFLOWER, see *CENTAUREA*

COTTON LAVENDER, see *SANTOLINA*

CROCOSMIA, see *MONTBRETIA*

CURRY PLANT, see *HELICHRYSUM* (*H. angustifolium*)

CUPID'S DART, see *CATANANCHE*

CYTISUS
BROOM

Mostly deciduous but some evergreen shrubs growing up to 8 feet high (2½ metres) with pea-like flowers of white, yellow or purple along the stems in April and May. Pick just before the top flowers are open and dry in desiccants for two or three days, or hang. If

CHOISYA:
MEXICAN ORANGE:
see page 23

25

tied in a circle the stem will take on an attractive curved shape.

DAHLIA   Perennial

Tuberous plants of a large range of colour and form, growing 2 to 4 feet high (60 to 120 cm), and flowering from August until cut down by frost. Only the cactus, pompom and small decorative types dry. Pick when as fully out as possible before the back petals fade and hang singly in a warm temperature.

DELPHINIUM
DELPHINIUM   Perennial

Blue, purple, mauve or white spurred flowers on spikes 4 to 6 feet high (120 to 180 cm) in June and July. Pick when as fully out as possible before the lower flowers have faded or dropped. Remove the leaves and hang separately. Do not attempt to dry if the lower flowers have started to drop—you can get an indication as to when this is likely to happen as seedheads will start to form in the lower florets. The side-shoots can also be bunched and dried once they are in flower.

See also next entry.

DELPHINIUM
LARKSPUR   Annual

Pink, blue, mauve, rose or white flowers growing on spikes 2 to 3 feet tall (60 to 90 cm). Better and earlier blooms are obtained by sowing in September; either sow seeds into the open ground and then thin out 6 to 9 inches apart (15 to 22 cm), or sow in pots under glass and plant out in the following spring. Alternatively, they can be sown where they are to flower from March to May and then thinned out. Pick when the flower is as fully out as possible, before the lower flowers fade or drop,

ECHINOPS:
GLOBE THISTLE:
see facing page

and hang separately. They can be bought from most florists but if you intend drying them, allow them to open further in water first. Once the flowers start falling, there is no point in trying to dry them. They are invaluable in all arrangements.

See also previous entry.

DIANTHUS
CARNATION   Perennial

Carnations do not dry well by hanging, but all, large or small, can be dried in desiccants for four to five days. Pick when fully in bloom so that the desiccant can reach all parts of the flower.

DIDISCUS—*D. caerulea*   Annual

Tiny lavender-blue flowers in clustered heads on stems 1½-2 feet tall (45 to 60 cm), in July to September. Hang to dry or treat in desiccants. The leaves press well.

DIGITALIS
FOXGLOVE   Biennial, perennial

The seedheads both of the wild and cultivated species dry well. Gather when they are first formed and before they turn brown, to retain their green colour. Remove leaves and hang. The plant also glycerines well.

DROPWORT, see *SPIRAEA*

ECHINOPS
GLOBE THISTLE   Perennial

Global heads of steel-blue spikes on stems 3 to 4 feet high (90 to 120 cm), with green-grey leaves, flowering in July and August. These

ERYNGIUM:
SEA HOLLY:
see page 28

have to be watched daily in order to pick them when the spikes are at their most blue but before the tiny blue flower appears. They will fall if picked once the first flower shows. Remove the leaves, which can be pressed, and hang.

For an illustration, see page 26.

ELEPHANT'S EAR, see *BERGENIA*

ERYNGIUM
SEA HOLLY   Perennial

There are several species of this plant, most with steel-blue, teasel-like heads, some larger than others, and they all dry well. The most common is *E. tripartitum*, which has sprays of small blue flowers in July and August. Pick when as many flowers as possible have turned blue, and hang. This dries very easily even without heat.

For an illustration, see previous page.

EUCALYPTUS

Fast-growing trees or large evergreen shrubs with glaucous, blue-grey leaves, roundish when young and narrower when adult. Pick sprays at any stage, hammer the ends of the stems and treat in glycerine for four to five weeks. They turn a lovely pinkish-blue colour.

EUPHORBIA—E. robbiae
SPURGE   Perennial

E. robbiae is perhaps the most common of the large species of Euphorbia to be grown in gardens, especially as ground cover in the shade. It has dark green, leathery leaves and greenish-yellow flowers on stems $1\frac{1}{2}$ feet long (45 cm) in May to July. Pick when the flowers are fully matured and hang in bunches. The

EUPHORBIA:
SPURGE

28

clusters of leaves are very useful in any arrangement and the flower bracts remain a lovely green (though they fade to a creamy colour if put in too much light). Alternatively, wait till they turn a reddish colour, in late summer, and then pick and treat in the same way. Euphorbia can also be glycerined. It turns a golden-brown colour if treated for a week to ten days. The white milky substance which comes from the base of the stems may cause an allergic reaction, so keep away from bare skin.

EVENING PRIMROSE, see *OENOTH-ERA*

EVERLASTING PEA, see *LATHYRUS*

FENNEL, see next section

FERNS, see next section

FEVERFEW, see *CHRYSANTHEMUM*

FILIPENDULA, see MEADOWSWEET in the next section

FLOSS FLOWER, see *AGERATUM*

FOXGLOVE, see *DIGITALIS*

GAILLARDIA
BLANKET FLOWER   Perennial

Yellow and red, daisy-like flowers on slender stems 1 to 2 feet tall (30 to 60 cm) with toothed leaves, flowering from June to September.

GAILLARDIA:
BLANKET FLOWER

Only the browny-red seedheads dry, but these should be gathered as soon as they are fully formed—otherwise they will drop. They dry easily if hung in bunches.

GALEGA
GOAT'S RUE   Perennial

Bushy plant growing 4 or 5 feet high (120 to 150 cm) with clusters of pea-shaped, mauve-white flowers in June and July, and little divided leaves. Pick when fully in flower (it does not seem to matter if some of the tiny flowers have already fallen) and hang. They turn a dull blue colour.

The foliage alone is also useful as it remains a good green.

GENTIANA
GENTIAN

There are several species of gentian, but the two varieties that dry best are *G. acaulis* and *G. sino-ornata*. Both have vivid blue, trumpet-like flowers on short stems; the former flowers in spring and the latter in September. Treat in desiccants for two or three days. The short stems need to be wired.

The graceful Willow Gentian (*G. asclepiadea*), which has smaller trumpet-like flowers along a slender stem in late July, sometimes dries satisfactorily if its leaves are stripped and it is then hung to dry in a very good heat.

GERANIUM, see *PELARGONIUM*

GLOBE AMARANTH, see *GOMPHRENA*

GLOBE ARTICHOKE, see next section

GALEGA:
GOAT'S RUE

GLOBE THISTLE, see *ECHINOPS*

GOAT'S BEARD, see *ARUNCUS*

GOAT'S RUE, see *GALEGA*

GOLDEN GARLIC, see *ALLIUM*

GOLDEN ROD, see *SOLIDAGO*

GOMPHRENA—G. globosa
GLOBE AMARANTH Annual

Orange, yellow, white, purple and pink ovoid flowers growing on erect stems 12 inches tall (30 cm) from July to September. The leaves are light green and hairy. Sow seeds under glass in March, prick out when large enough to handle and plant out in a sunny position in May. Cut just before the flowers are fully open and hang in bunches.

GRAPE HYACINTH, see *MUSCARI*

GRASSES, see next section

GREVILLEA, see next section

GYPSOPHILA Perennial

The best for drying is *G. paniculata* var. 'Bristol Fairy'. It has tiny white flowers on branching stems 2 or 3 feet tall (60 to 90 cm) in summer. It dries very easily, either upright in containers or hung. There is also an annual form, but it is rather short and not worth the trouble for drying.

GOMPHRENA:
GLOBE AMARANTH

31

1 *A formal arrangement in blues, pinks and silver, 65 cm (26 inches) high, with delphiniums as the main feature*

A   *Delphinium*
B   *Zinnia*
C   *Peony*
D   *Rose (spray)*
E   *Stachys lanata*
      (Lamb's Tongue)
F   *Echinops*

G   *Chrysanthemum*
      ('Wirral Double')
H   *Poppy seedheads*
I   *Larkspur*
J   *Astilbe*
K   *Dahlia*
L   *Polygonum Bistorta*

M   *Artemisia*
N   *Scabious leaf*
O   *Senecio maritima*
      (Sea Ragwort)
P   *Cornflower*
Q   *Bergenia*

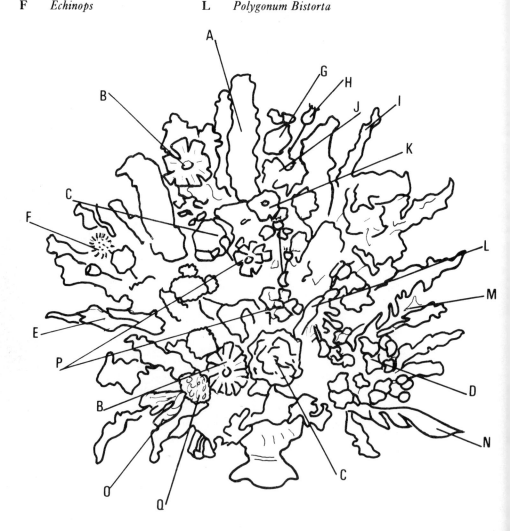

2 *A small formal arrangement, 45 cm (18 inches) high, mainly in yellows*

A *Solidago (Golden Rod)*
B *Zinnia*
C *Marigold*
D *Dahlia*
E *Heliopsis*
F *Helichrysum bracteatum*
  (Straw Flower)

G *Fern*
H *Santolina*
I *Peony*
J *Thalictrum leaf*
K *Hosta leaf*
L *Euphorbia robbiae*
  (Spurge)

M *Achillea 'Moonshine'*
N *Limonium*
  (Sea Lavender, Statice)
O *Rose*

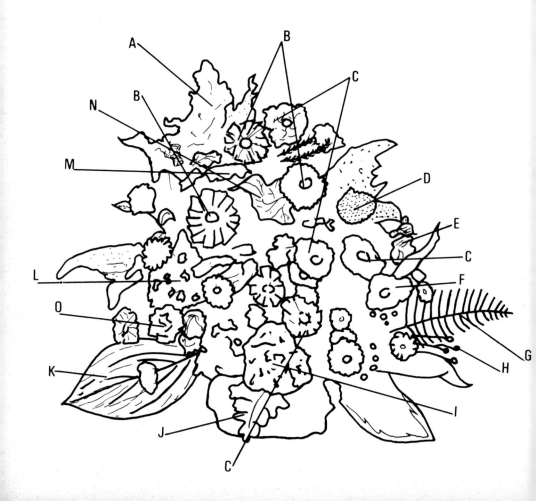

3 *The rose tree, standing about 35 cm (15 inches) high, is covered with polyanthus roses set in a bed of hydrangea. The basket, which is about 30 cm (13 inches) high, provides a less formal arrangement.*

A   Rose
B   Cornflower
C   Zinnia
D   Polygonum Bistorta
    (Snakeweed)
E   Rose (spray of
    'Dorothy Perkins')

F   Larkspur
G   Nigella seedheads
    (Love-in-a-Mist)
H   Acroclinium
I   Helichrysum bracteatum
    (Straw Flower)

J   Thalictrum leaf
K   Limonium
    (Sea Lavender, Statice)

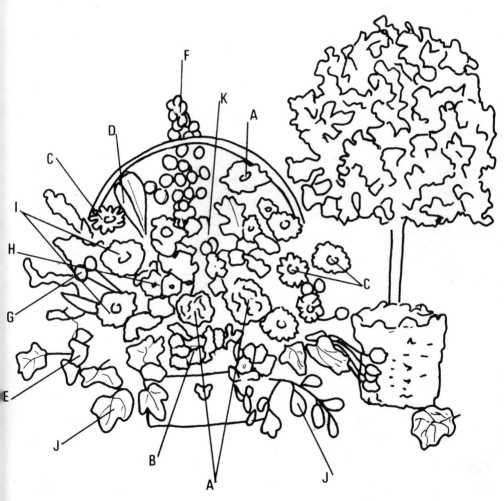

HEATHS and HEATHERS, see the next section

HEBE Perennial

There are many species of this half-hardy evergreen shrub, varying in size and in flowering time. Dense spikes of flowers—mauve, pink or white—are borne between July and October. Pick when almost fully out and hang to dry. Stems of leaves alone can be glycerined.

HELICHRYSUM—H. bracteatum
STRAW FLOWER Annual

Many-coloured, double, daisy-like flowers with papery bracts and lance-shaped leaves. Sow under glass in February or March and plant on, or sow straight into the ground in a sunny position in April. Invaluable in any dried flower arrangement. To get perfection it is important to pick when only the outer bracts are open. If the flower is picked when the yellow centre is showing, it will dry overblown and unattractive. Begin by picking only the head of the terminal flower and insert a wire up into its centre—this should be done immediately, as once the head dries it is hard to insert the wire. As it dries—upright in a container—the wire will become firm.

During the season side-shoots will develop on the plant. The flowers can be treated in the same way or, after removing the leaves, can be dried on their stems, by hanging them in bunches.

HELICHRYSUM—H. angustifolium
CURRY PLANT Perennial

A half-hardy shrub which has clusters of small yellow flowers borne from June to August on stems 1 to 1½ feet tall (30 to 45 cm) with thin,

HELICHRYSUM:
STRAW FLOWER

strong-smelling, white, downy leaves. Either gather stems when first in flower, or leave a little before picking—in which case they become fluffy on drying, which looks most attractive. Hang in bunches.

HELIOPSIS   Perennial

Single or double, golden-yellow, daisy-like flowers borne on erect stems 3 to 4 feet tall (90 to 120 cm) with mid-green lanceolate leaves, in July and August. The double variety ('Golden Plume') dries very well. Pick stems of varying lengths, both long and short, choosing some flowers which are fully open and some in bud. They are very useful in an arrangement, both for the back and at the front. The leaves remain a good green colour and need not be stripped.

For an illustration, see overleaf.

HELIPTERUM, see *ACROCLINIUM* and *RHODANTHE*

HELLEBORUS
HELLEBORE   Perennial

H. niger, the Christmas Rose, has a white saucer-shaped flower with a yellow centre and dark evergreen leaves, and blooms December to March; *H. orientalis*, the Lenten Rose, has a variable pink, purple, white or cream flower on a stem up to 15 inches tall (45 cm), blooming February to April. The seedheads of both dry well. Pick when the seedhead has formed and leave to dry in a warm room.

H. corsicus has pale green, cup-shaped flowers on large trusses 2 to 3 feet high (60 to 90 cm) with large evergreen leaves, January to April. *H. foetidus* is similar, but with narrow,

HELICHRYSUM:
CURRY PLANT:
see facing page

35

lanceolate leaves and smaller, bell-shaped flowers. The individual florets dry well in desiccants if picked when fully out and treated for three to four days.

Some people may be allergic to the white sap issuing from hellebore stems when cut, so treat with care.

HOLLYHOCK, see *ALTHAEA*

HONESTY, see *LUNARIA*

HOP, see next section

HORNBEAM, see next section

HOSTA   Perennial

Clumps of attractive foliage in all shades of green and varying sizes according to condition, growing from May to October. Lilac and white flowers are borne on spikes 1 to $1\frac{1}{2}$ feet tall (30 to 45 cm). Make sure the leaves are perfect and mature before pressing them, preferably between sheets of brown paper or blotting-paper to absorb the moisture. They keep a good colour.

HUMULUS, see HOP in the next section

HYDRANGEA

The common hydrangea, *H. macrophylla*, is a hardy shrub 4 to 6 feet high ($1\frac{1}{4}$ to $1\frac{3}{4}$ metres) with heads growing on previous year's growth, each composed of small star-shaped flowers in blue, mauve, pink and white, flowering from July till the first frosts. There is also *H. paniculata*, which has creamy-pink conical heads

HELIOPSIS:
see page 35

in August and September. Both these dry well, but the lace-cap hydrangea does not. I usually cut the heads only when they start changing colour and feel crisp to the touch, and then dry them upright or hang. They can be picked a little earlier, if desired, and dried off in a little water (which should not be topped up), but I have had more failures with this method. It is advisable not to pick the stem too long as this will prevent flowering the following year. When dry the head can be lengthened by inserting a florist's wire into the stem.

IVY, see next section

JERUSALEM SAGE, see *PHLOMIS*

KNAPWEED, see *CENTAUREA*

KNOTWEED, see *POLYGONUM*

KOCHIA—K. scoparia var. trichophila
BURNING BUSH   Annual

Bush 2 to 3 feet tall (60 to 90 cm) of fine green leaves which turn reddish-purple in late summer. Sow under glass in March and plant out in May or early June in a sunny position. Pick when a mature green, or when the leaves have changed or are changing colour, and hang.

LADY'S MANTLE, see *ALCHEMILLA*

LAMB'S EARS, LAMB'S TONGUE, see *STACHYS*

LARKSPUR, see *DELPHINIUM*

KOCHIA:
BURNING BUSH

37

LATRIS:
BLAZING STAR
see facing page

LATHYRUS—*L. latifolius*
EVERLASTING PEA　　　　Perennial

Climbing plant resembling the sweet pea with stems 6 to 7 feet long (1¾ to 2 metres) which die back in autumn, with pink, purple and white flowers from June to September. Pick stems when most of the flowers have opened and hang in bunches in a good heat. They dry a subtle bluish-mauve colour and are both unusual and useful in small arrangements.

LAVANDULA
LAVENDER

Small evergreen shrub up to 3 feet tall (1 metre) with fragrant purple-blue flower spikes in June to July. *Lavandula* 'Hidcote' has darker flowers and is most attractive when dried. Pick before the flowers are fully out, tie in bunches and dry either by hanging or upright. For the strongest fragrance, pick before the flowers open.

LAVATERA
TREE MALLOW　　　　　Annual

Shrubby plant 3 feet tall (90 cm) with pale purple, funnel-shaped flowers in clusters at the ends of small branches in July. There is also a biennial tree mallow which grows up to 10 feet high (3 metres). The seedheads of both dry well but picking and disentangling them is time-consuming. Leave till well-formed before gathering, though by then the weather may have taken its toll of several heads.

LAVENDER, see *LAVANDULA*

LAVENDER COTTON, see *SANTOLINA*

LEEKS, see next section

LENTEN ROSE, see *HELLEBORUS*

LIATRIS—L. spicata
BLAZING STAR   Perennial

Purple, closely-packed spikes 1 to $2\frac{1}{2}$ feet tall
(30 to 45 cm), flowering in July to August,
from the top downwards. The leaves are small
and lance-shaped. Pick when in full flower
and hang. They take a long time to dry out.

LILAC, see *SYRINGA*

LILY OF THE VALLEY, see *CONVAL-LARIA*

LIME, see next section

LIMONIUM
SEA LAVENDER, STATICE

L. sinuatum has sprays of pink, lavender, blue,
yellow and white everlasting flowers. Sow
under glass in early February and plant out in
a sunny position in May. Pick only when all
the flowers are fully out, and hang. Once
picked the flowers will not come out in water.
    L. Suworowii, often called Pink Pokers, has
rose-pink wavy spikes up to 10 inches long
(25 cm). Sow under glass in February to
March and plant out in a sunny position in
May. Pick when just in flower and hang. It
dries well. For an illustration of Pink Pokers,
see overleaf.
    L. latifolium (perennial) has lavender-blue
flowers on woody stems 2 feet tall (60 cm) in
June to August. Pick when fully out and hang.

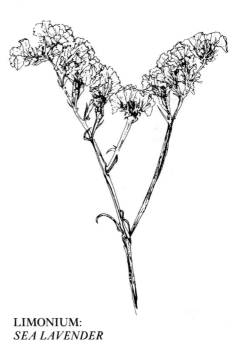

LIMONIUM:
SEA LAVENDER

39

LONICERA—*L. nitida*

Evergreen shrub with small leaves, often used for hedging, which grows both in the open and in shade. There is also a golden-leaved variety which grows best in the open. Sprays of both can be treated in glycerine for three to four weeks; they darken, but the golden lonicera is particularly attractive.

LOVE-IN-A-MIST, see *NIGELLA*

LOVE-LIES-BLEEDING, see *AMARANTHUS*

LUNARIA—*L. annua*
HONESTY   Biennial

Sprays of purple flowers with heart-shaped leaves in April to June, followed by silvery seedpods which can be dried. Pick in August when the centre layer is still covered by the outer brown layers, and hang. When they are dry, and you can hear the seeds rattle, the outer layers can be stripped easily to reveal a silvery transparent centre. Be sure to keep some of the seeds for the following year's crop if you do not leave some stems to seed naturally.

LUPINUS
LUPIN   Annual, perennial

Tall spikes flowering in June in colours ranging from white and yellow to pinks, deep reds and purple. If you can catch the moment when the flowers are fading and forming seedheads, and then pick them at once and hang, they will dry beautifully, leaving you with pale-coloured spikes. It is quite hard to achieve.

MACLEAYA, see *BOCCONIA*

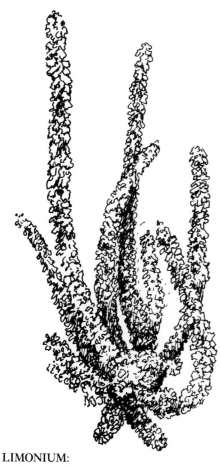

LIMONIUM:
STATICE
see page 39

40

MALLOW TREE, see *LAVATERA*

MARIGOLD: African, see *TAGETES*;
Pot, see *CALENDULA*

MASTERWORT, see *ASTRANTIA*

MATTHIOLA
STOCK   Annual, biennial

There are several kinds of stock but the only
ones that dry are the Brompton and Ten-
Weeks Stocks, and of these only the double
ones. The Brompton Stocks are 2 to 3 feet
high (60 to 90 cm) and the seeds should be
sown in June or July, for flowering the following spring and summer. The Ten-Week
Stocks are about 1½ feet high (45 cm). Sow in
February to March under glass and plant out
in May. Cut when most of the flowers are full,
and hang in bunches, or dry small stems in
desiccants for four to five days.

MEADOW RUE, see *THALICTRUM*

MEGASEA, see *BERGENIA*

MEXICAN ORANGE, see *CHOISYA*

MOCK ORANGE, see *PHILADELPHUS*

MOLUCCELLA—*M. laevis*
BELLS OF IRELAND,
SHELL FLOWER   Annual

Spikes 2 to 3 feet tall (60 to 90 cm) with pale
green leaves and bell-shaped bracts in which
small pinkish-white flowers appear in August

MOLUCCELLA:
BELLS OF IRELAND

to September. Sow under glass in March and plant out in a sunny position in May. Do not pick until flowers appear in most of the bells. Remove leaves and the top few bracts, and hang separately: they will remain a lovely pale green for some time but will eventually turn a parchment colour. If stood in a container with a little water, they will dry but their pale green fades more quickly. Alternatively, they can be treated in glycerine for three or four days and then hung to dry, and will turn a parchment colour but remain supple and last for years.

MOLY, see *ALLIUM*

MONTBRETIA
syn. CROCOSMIA

Perennial

Yellow to deep orange, tubular flowers on stems 1½ to 2 feet tall (45 to 60 cm), growing from corms, August to September. The leaves are upright and sword-shaped. Gather the seedheads as soon as they are fully formed but still green, and either hang or dry upright. The leaves press well.

MUSCARI—M. botryoides
GRAPE HYACINTH

This bulb produces in spring bright blue or white, closely-packed, tiny bells on cylindrical heads on stems 4 to 6 inches tall (10 to 15 cm). The leaves are grass-like. Either wait until the green seedheads have formed, and then pick and dry upright in a container, or leave in the garden until the seedheads have become papery and cream in colour. In the latter case, select only perfect specimens as they are inclined to get damaged by the weather.

MONTBRETIA

NEPETA—N. Cataria
CATMINT   Perennial

So called because its fragrance seems to attract cats. Soft, lavender-coloured flowers growing in whorls on stems 1 to 1½ feet tall (30 to 45 cm), from May to September. The leaves are small, serrated and grey-green. Cut when as fully out as possible before the top florets fade, and hang in bunches. This is invaluable for use as 'filler' in the centre of an arrangement.

NIGELLA
LOVE-IN-A-MIST   Annual

Mixed shades of blue, rose-pink or white flowers nestling in collars of fennel-like leaves on stems 18 inches tall (45 cm). Sow seeds either in March or April where they are to flower, or in September for a crop the following summer. Thin the seedlings to 9 inches apart (about 25 cm). Pick the flowers as soon as they open, bunch with all their heads level, and hang. When arranging, use in bunches as this is more effective; single flowers would be insignificant.

    Love-in-a-Mist seedheads are also very useful in an arrangement and some take on a lovely purple hue. Gather in late summer when well formed but before they begin to turn brown or are spoiled by the weather. Remove most of the lower leaves and hang.

OENOTHERA—O. biennis
EVENING PRIMROSE   Biennial

A profusion of pale yellow flowers borne on stems 3 feet tall (90 cm), from June to October, with mid-green, lanceolate leaves. They seed very easily. The seedheads, if

OENOTHERA:
EVENING PRIMROSE

picked when well formed and still green, make attractive outlines.

ONIONS, see next section

ONOPORDON
THISTLE   Biennial

Very tall, up to 6 or 8 feet ($1\frac{3}{4}$ to $2\frac{1}{2}$ metres), with branching and winged stems and silvery-grey leaves. The flower is pale purple and thistle-like, appearing in July and August. Cut stems when the flower is well open and hang or dry upright, for large arrangements.

PAMPAS GRASS, see next section

PAPAVER
POPPY   Annual, perennial

The seedheads both of wild poppies and of cultivated ones dry well by hanging, but the annual variety are prettier. They all seed readily. Pick when the seedheads are fully formed but before they turn brown or are spoiled by the weather.

PEARL EVERLASTING, see *ANA-PHALIS*

PELARGONIUM
GERANIUM

If you do not mind sacrificing the flowers at their best when bedded out in a formal setting, the double geraniums dry and preserve their colour well. Pick when fully in flower and hang. The bright pillarbox red is not the easiest of colours to put with other flowers in an arrangement, but pinks are most attractive.

PHLOMIS:
JERUSALEM SAGE
see facing page

44

PEONIA
PEONY
Perennial

Large showy flowers in many shades of pink to red, yellow and white, flowering on stems 1½ to 2 feet tall (45 to 60 cm) in May to June. The leaves are of irregular size and shape, some lobed and some not.

Only the double peonies dry. Cut the flowers when just open but not full-blown, and hang in good heat. They take some time to dry. Make sure the stem is hard and dry right up near the flower. The red peonies are difficult to dry, but the pink variety, 'Sarah Bernhardt', is easier.

The leaves press well.

PHILADELPHUS—P. coronarius
MOCK ORANGE

Tall deciduous shrubs up to 10 feet high (3 metres) with single or double, white, fragrant, cup-like flowers in June and July. Only the double varieties dry satisfactorily. Cut sprays with as many blooms as possible, remove leaves and either hang or dry upright. They are useful for inserting in the centre of an arrangement, allowing the creamy flowers to peep out and give lightness.

Small sprays also dry well in desiccants for four to five days, though in time the flowers turn cream.

PHLOMIS—P. fruticosa
JERUSALEM SAGE

Evergreen shrub up to 4 feet tall (120 cm) bearing grey-green leaves on spreading branches with deep yellow flowers in whorls at their ends in June and July. Gather when the flowers are full, bunch together and hang. The seedheads also dry easily once the flowers have fallen.

For an illustration, see facing page.

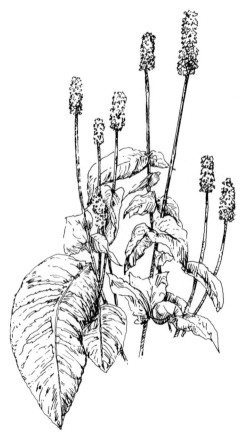

POLYGONUM:
KNOTWEED
see page 46

PHYSALIS—*P. Franchetii*
CAPE GOOSEBERRY,
CHINESE LANTERN

Annual, perennial

Small, white, insignificant flowers which turn first to green and then to inflated orange fruits. Pick when the lowest lanterns are just turning colour and the top ones are still green. Remove the leaves, and hang in bunches or dry upright. The fruits can be cut down the 'creases' and folded back to make petals for Christmas decorations. They can also be painted if the bright orange does not fit in with other colour schemes.

PINK POKERS, see *LIMONIUM*

PLUME POPPY, see *BOCCONIA*

POLYGONATUM
SOLOMON'S SEAL

Small, white, bell-like flowers hanging on arching stems 2 to 3 feet tall (60 to 90 cm), tucked under leaves which are long and oval. Allow the leaves to mature as long as possible, but watch that they are not attacked by caterpillars before picking. The quicker they are dried, the better the leaves will hold their colour and shape. They can also be pressed.

POLYGONUM
KNOTWEED

Perennial

All polygonums dry well. *P. amplexicaule* has red flower spikes starting to flower in June and continuing through into the autumn. The deep green leaves are heart-shaped and pointed. *P. Bistorta* (Snakeweed) has soft pink spikes 3 feet long (90 cm) in May and June, with oblong or oval leaves. The small varieties,

RHODANTHE:
see facing page

46

especially *P. affine* 'Donald Lowndes' which has a dense mat of evergreen leaves and flowers 4 to 6 inches in size (10 to 15 cm), dry very well and are useful for small arrangements. Pick when flowers are full, remove all leaves and hang in bunches.

P. baldschuanicum (Russian Vine) is a very fast-growing climber which grows up to 40 feet (12 metres) and is very useful for screening purposes. It has pale green, ovate leaves and pale pink or white flowers hanging in panicles 10 to 18 inches across (25 to 45 cm). Dries well if gathered when first in flower, and hung.

For an illustration, see page 45.

POPPY, see *PAPAVER*

POT MARIGOLD, see *CALENDULA*

RHODANTHE syn. HELIPTERUM
R. Manglesii   Annual

Rose-pink or white, straw-textured, daisy-like flowers on slender stems 12 inches tall (30 cm) from July to August. The leaves are oblong and glaucous. Sow under glass in March and then plant on, or sow straight into the open ground in a sunny position in April. Pick just as the buds begin to open. Remove most of the leaves, tie in bunches and hang. If the flowers are left to open fully they fade and will be unattractive when dried.

For an illustration, see facing page.
See also *ACROCLINIUM*.

ROSA
ROSE

Only double roses dry, both by hanging, when they shrink a little, and in desiccants.

When dried by the hanging method they

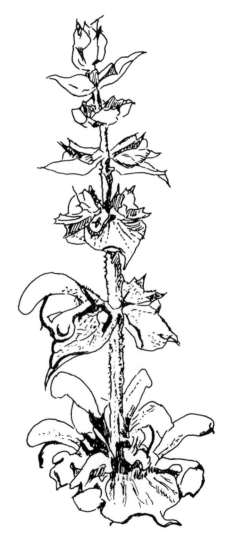

SALVIA:
SAGE
see page 48

47

should be cut in dry weather when just open, though not in full bloom, so that the warmth and air can get to all parts of the flower. If there is moisture on the petals, or at the base of the flower, they will turn brown and fall. Roughly speaking, the least satisfactory are those which have long buds, e.g. 'Queen Elizabeth'. Of the floribunda roses, 'Elizabeth of Glamis' and 'Pink Parfait' dry well, both singly and in sprays. Of the hybrid teas, 'Peace' and 'Super Star' are both good. The old double musk roses, which will retain some of their perfume, also dry well, but it is hard to pick them at the right time as the flowers open so quickly in sun and seem to fall again almost at once. The old polyanthus roses, e.g. 'The Fairy', dry very well, as do the sprays of many shrub roses, even if some flowers are still in bud. Usually, though, single buds do not dry well by the hanging method.

To dry in desiccants, pick when just open and treat for three or four days. Buds can also be treated in this way, but will take longer.

ROSMARINUS—R. officinalis
ROSEMARY

Narrow, shiny, aromatic leaves on a bush about 4 feet high (120 cm) with lavender flowers appearing in summer. Treat in glycerine for two or three weeks when the stems turn a silvery-grey and the leaves hold their fragrance.

SAGE, see SALVIA

SALVIA
SAGE   Perennial

There are a number of sages, most with violet-purple or blue spiked flowers growing on stems 2 to 3 feet tall (60 to 90 cm) from July to September. Cut either when the flower

SANTOLINA:
COTTON LAVENDER
see facing page

is full, or just as the flowers are over when the seedheads still retain their mauve-blue tinge. Strip the leaves and hang. They dry quickly.

S. Horminum, which is an annual, is shown as 'Clary' in some seed catalogues. It is a bushy plant $1\frac{1}{2}$ to 2 feet tall (45 to 60 cm) which has branched stems and terminal bracts coloured pink, white and purple, in June to September. Cut the flowers when the bracts are mature and brightly coloured, and hang. They dry well and the colour lasts a long time.

For an illustration, see page 47.

SAND FLOWER, see *AMMOBIUM*

SANTOLINA
COTTON LAVENDER

Bushy, evergreen shrub with silvery-grey foliage, and button-like, yellow flowers on long, thin stems in July. Cut the stems when fully out but before turning brown, and hang in bunches. They should be used in bunches in arrangements rather than singly.

For an illustration, see facing page.

SATIN FLOWER, see *SISYRINCHIUM*

SCILLA—S. campanulata, S. non-scripta
BLUEBELL

Large bluebells in white, pink, pale and dark blue. When the creamy-white seedheads have formed and are crisp to the touch, pick the perfect ones before the weather spoils them. The hollow stem can be wired and bent to the required shape.

SEA HOLLY, see *ERYNGIUM*

STACHYS:
LAMB'S TONGUE
see page 51

49

SEA LAVENDER, see *LIMONIUM*

SEA RAGWORT, see *SENECIO*

SENECIO—S. Maritima
SEA RAGWORT

Half-hardy shrub with deeply lobed, silvery leaves, and small yellow flowers appearing from July to September. The foliage, which is the plant's main attraction, dries well if picked when mature. Make sure the leaves are clean and unspoiled by the weather. Hang.

SHASTA DAISY, see *CHRYSANTHE-MUM*

SHELL FLOWER, see *MOLUCCELLA*

SISYRINCHIUM—S. striatum
SATIN FLOWER

Sword-shaped leaves with stems carrying creamy-yellow, star-like flowers in June and July. Pick the seedheads when they are green and either hang, or treat in glycerine for about a week.

SNEEZEWORT, see *ACHILLEA*

SOLIDAGO
GOLDEN ROD   Perennial

Sprays of yellow, mimosa-like flowers borne on stems 2 to 4 feet high (60 to 120 cm) in August to September. Cut when as fully out as possible before the top flowers turn brown, and dry upright or hang. They dry very quickly.

TAMARIX:
TAMARISK
see page 53

SOLOMON'S SEAL, see *POLYGONA-TUM*

SPIRAEA

There are many species and most dry well. *S. Bumalda* ('Anthony Waterer') is a small, deciduous shrub about 3 feet high (90 cm) with deep pink, flat flowerheads in July and August. Cut the flowerhead when the majority of the florets are in full bloom, and hang. It dries rather a dull pink but is useful in the centre of an arrangement. *S. lobata, syn. Filipendula rubra* ('Queen of the Prairie') has deep pink, feathery plumed flowers and large, lobed, deep green leaves, and blooms in July and August. Pick when the plumes are well in flower and before fading, and dry upright. *S. filipendula* (Dropwort) grows to a height of 2 or 3 feet (60 to 90 cm). It has mid-green palmate leaves and creamy-white plumes, flowering in July and August. Pick the sprays as near fully out as possible before any florets turn brown, strip the leaves and dry upright.

See also *ARUNCUS*.

SPURGE, see *EUPHORBIA*

STACHYS—S. lanata
LAMB'S TONGUE, LAMB'S EARS
Perennial

Grey-green, felt-like leaved plant which produces mauve-flowered spikes 1 to 1½ feet tall (30 to 45 cm) in June to July. Pick as soon as the small flowers have appeared—not before. Remove any leaves that have been spoiled by the weather, and hang to dry. If the spikes are picked before they are fully grown, they do not dry firm, but are still invaluable in an arrangement.

For an illustration, see page 49.

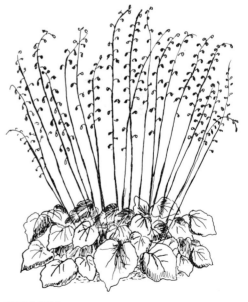

TELLIMA
see page 53

STATICE, see *LIMONIUM*

STOCK, see *MATTHIOLA*

STRAW FLOWER, see *HELICHRYSUM*

STRAWBERRY TREE, see *ARBUTUS*

SYRINGA
LILAC

Deciduous shrub or small tree up to 20 feet high (6 metres) bearing single and double flowers in large panicles, in colours of white, pink, mauve and purple. The mauve varieties dry if picked when first in full flower in May and June, and hung. The white turns an unattractive brown. Alternatively, leave the seedheads to dry on the tree and then gather them. Lilac also dries well in a desiccant and should be treated for four to five days.

The name 'Syringa' is sometimes used for the Mock Orange as well; this will be found under its botanical name, *PHILADELPHUS*.

TAGETES—T. erecta
AFRICAN MARIGOLD   Annual

Large yellow, golden or orange flowers on vigorous plants $1\frac{1}{2}$ to 2 feet tall (45 to 60 cm), throughout the summer. Pick when the flower is fully out—especially the centre. The air is then able to reach all parts and it will dry well, though slowly, if hung in a warm atmosphere. Make sure to pick in dry weather, otherwise some petals will turn brown on drying. The stems should be picked short, so as to preserve and encourage the ensuing buds, and should then be wired (push a wire up the hollow stem). Marigolds can also be treated in desiccants for four or five days.

THALICTRUM:
MEADOW RUE
see facing page

52

TAMARIX
TAMARISK

Small and numerous pink flowers on loose-growing branches with feathery leaves, often seen near the sea. Cut the sprays as they are coming into flower in August, and hang to dry.

For an illustration, see page 50.

TELLIMA   Perennial

Tiny, green, pink-tinged, bell-like flowers growing along thin erect stems $1\frac{1}{2}$ to 2 feet tall (45 to 60 cm) out of a bed of maple-shaped leaves from April to June. Pick when the flowers on the stem are as fully out as possible, bunch and hang. It is better to group a number of stems together in an arrangement than to use them individually. The leaves turn a reddish colour and can be picked and pressed at any stage.

For an illustration, see page 51.

THALICTRUM
MEADOW RUE   Perennial

There are several species. *T. aquilegiifolium* is 2 to 3 feet high (60 to 90 cm) and has pinkish-purple flowers in panicles in May to June, and *T. lucidum*, which is most common, has fluffy yellow flowers growing 4 to 5 feet high (60 to 90 cm) in July and August. Both dry well if picked when the flowers are just out, and hung. The leaves resemble maidenhair fern and can be pressed.

For an illustration, see facing page.

THISTLE, see *ECHINOPS*, *ONOPORDON*

THYME, see *THYMUS*

XERANTHEMUM
see page 54

53

THYMUS
THYME

The common thyme (*T. vulgaris*) has dark green, aromatic, long, narrow leaves. The clusters of mauve flowers dry well if picked when fully out, and hung. Sprays of lemon thyme and some of the small alpine varieties can be pressed and used in small arrangements. Remove some of the basal leaves first.

TREE MALLOW, see *LAVATERA*

VERBASCUM   Biennial

There are several species and their seedheads all dry well. Wait until the seedheads are set on the plant and then pick and hang. They seed readily.

WISTERIA

Deciduous climber with mauve or white pea-like flowers in pendulous racemes in May and early June. The leaves are pinnate, each with twelve or more leaflets, and can be pressed for about a month (they are very delicate, and if pressed for too long the leaflets will break away from the stem). The flowers will dry well by hanging if picked when first in bloom.

XERANTHEMUM   Annual

Small, single or double, daisy-like flowers in mauve, lilac, pink or white. Sow in March or April out of doors in a sunny position. Pick when the flowers are barely open, bunch and hang. Use the flowers in bunches when arranging rather than individually.

For an illustration, see previous page.

YARROW, see *ACHILLEA*

ZINNIA   Annual

Single or double, daisy-like flowers in a variety of colours including red, yellow, orange, white, purple and green on stems $1\frac{1}{2}$ to 3 feet tall (60 to 90 cm). These dry very well in desiccants. Sow in March to April under glass and transfer to pots when large enough to handle. Plant out in June. Cut the flowers when fully open, picking only down to the next shoot to encourage further flowering, and dry face down in desiccants for two or three days. They can then be lengthened by inserting wire into the hollow stems.

Appendix

OTHER PLANT MATERIAL FOR DRYING

There are, of course, many other sources you can try in search of plant material which will dry well—the vegetable garden, hedgerows and waysides, even house plants. The following supplementary list includes wild flowers, herbs, foliage, etc. It is well worth experimenting with any other plants which appeal to you.

BAMBOO

Pick first year's growth in the autumn while the leaves are still green and unaffected by weather, and dry upright. Sprays of leaves can also be pressed. They stay a good green colour.

BAY

Treat sprays of bay in glycerine solution for about two weeks. The leaves will turn a dark olive green colour.

BEECH

Cut sprays in July to September and treat in glycerine for one to two weeks or until all the leaves have absorbed the solution. The earlier the sprays are picked, the darker the leaves will become. Remove any damaged leaves before treating and split the bottom of the stem as well.

BOX

Dark green or variegated, small, leathery-leaved tree or shrub often used for hedging and therefore clipped back. The small branches of a free-growing tree glycerine well if picked when the sprays are not too old. The wood of mature branches is too hard to absorb the glycerine.

BRACKEN

Take care to find perfect green specimens, then pick when mature. These can either be pressed for four or five weeks, when they will retain their colour, or glycerined for two weeks, in which case they will turn a light brown colour and curl quite gracefully. For ferns, see overleaf.

BULRUSH

Long, brown-flowered, poker-like spikes usually growing in marshy land or beside a lake or pond. Pick before fully developed and either hang or dry upright.

BUTTERCUP

Gather these when in full flower in May and hang in bunches in a warm room.

CARROT

The leaf will dry well if gathered when fully mature and hung. It gives a light feathery touch to small arrangements.

CHIVES, see LEEK

DOCK and SORREL

To be found on waste land and in the hedgerows. The whorl-shaped seedheads, green in spring and turning to a lovely red colour, can be dried by hanging. Pick whenever possible as long as the seeds have not started to fall. They can also be treated in glycerine for one to two weeks and will turn a beautiful dark red colour.

FENNEL

Small yellow flowers borne in umbels on stems 5 to 8 feet tall ($1\frac{1}{2}$ to $2\frac{1}{2}$ metres) in July and August. The feathery leaves may be used fresh or dried for flavouring. When seedheads have formed, remove leaves (which can be pressed) and hang or dry upright. The aromatic smell still lingers a little even after the stems have been dried.

FERNS

Ferns of all sorts can be dried by pressing and they retain their colour well. Make sure that they are lying in their natural curves with none of the fronds overlapping. Six weeks is a recommended time.

FOXGLOVE, see *DIGITALIS* in the Glossary section.

GLOBE ARTICHOKE

If you fail to cut the artichoke when ready for eating, the large purple flowerheads that will form dry well as long as they are picked as soon as they appear. Strip the leaves and prickles. They take a long time to dry, either by hanging or upright. If they are picked too late and the powder-puff seeds fall, the head can still look attractive in a large arrangement.

GRASSES

The list of grasses is innumerable and all can be dried, either upright or hanging or flat, depending on the shape and size. If the stem is delicate, it is better to hang or dry flat. Pick any attractive heads of grass you see, either in the garden or by the roadside, but make sure they are in their prime. They add lightness and interest to any arrangement.

GREVILLEA

The foliage of this pot plant glycerines well. Leave in the solution for about a week.

HEATHS AND HEATHERS

There are a vast number of heaths (*Erica*) or

heathers (*Calluna*). The only ones that dry satisfactorily are the double ones (e.g. 'H.E. Beale' which has double pink flowers) and those that have a 'dry' appearance to the leaf and flower. These need no treatment other than to be left to dry out in a container with a little water, which should not be topped up. They can be dried in glycerine (for two or three days) when they retain their bells but turn brown and unattractive.

HOP

Both the wild hop found in hedgerows and the cultivated annual (*Humulus*) can be dried. Gather while the flowers are young and green. Remove the leaves and hang. They dry easily.

HORNBEAM

Tree or hedge, similar to beech but with mid-green, ovate, prominently veined, double-toothed leaves. The female catkins appear in April to May and are followed by hanging clusters of winged bracts. Cut sprays or small branches in June to July when they are well-formed, remove all leaves and stand in glycerine solution for three or four weeks, after splitting the base of all stems. They turn a lovely, dark lime colour.

IVY

Ivy can either be pressed for six weeks, or treated in glycerine for about three weeks after giving the leaves a preliminary sponging with the solution; alternatively, immerse completely. If glycerined, it will darken.

LEEKS, ONIONS, CHIVES

Leeks and onions can be left to flower where sown or planted out for ordinary purposes, or

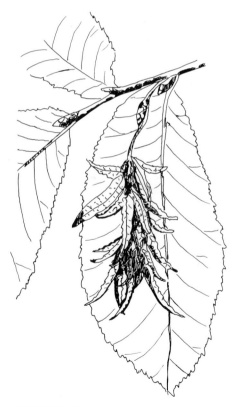

HORNBEAM

57

they can be planted in a separate bed. If left in the ground they may flower a second year. Pick when the flowers have opened and hang or dry upright. Leeks are the more satisfactory as they have firm stems but take a long time to dry out. Onion heads also dry but it is better to remove them from their hollow stems and put them on florist's wire. Chives have mauve flowers which appear in June to July, and should be picked when fully out.

Leeks, onions and chives all lose their smell on drying.

For the ornamental *Alliums*, see the Glossary section.

LIME

Tall straight trees with smooth bark and heart-shaped, tooth-edged leaves appearing in May. They have small, sweet-smelling, white flowers which are succeeded by small round fruits. Cut sprays when the fruits are well-formed towards the end of July to August. Remove leaves and treat in glycerine solution for three to four weeks. They remain a lovely, lime green colour, but darken slightly.

MEADOWSWEET

This plant, found in damp ditches and around ponds, has branching, creamy-white heads in June to August, growing to a height of 2 or 3 feet (60 to 90 cm). The leaves are fern-like. Pick when first in full flower, before the florets start turning brown, and dry upright.

NIPPLEWORT

Seen growing in hedgerows, this plant has small yellow heads borne in loose clusters from May to October. Gather when the seed-heads have formed and hang or dry upright.

ONION, see LEEK

PAMPAS GRASS

Silky cream plumes, $1\frac{1}{2}$ to 2 feet long (45 to 60 cm), flowering on stems 6 to 9 feet tall ($1\frac{3}{4}$ to $2\frac{3}{4}$ metres), in late summer. The leaves are glaucous, arching and rough-edged. Cut plumes while still young, and hang. Clumps of leaves can also be gathered in the autumn, bound very tightly and hung. They dry in corkscrew shapes and are effective in large arrangements.

POPPY, see *PAPAVER* in the Glossary

SORREL, see DOCK

SWEETCORN

The seedheads can be cut at any time once the cob has set as long as they are fully formed. Strip off the outer leaves and dry upright.

58

Colours

The following lists give the colours of seedheads, foliage and flowers mentioned in this book, together with an indication of the months of flowering. 'A' denotes an Annual. Italicized entries will be found in the Glossary, non-italicized entries in the Appendix.

Foliage

Arbutus (Strawberry Tree), dark green
Artemisia, silver
Bamboo, green
Bay, dark green
Beech, dark green/dark bronze
Box, dark green fading to parchment
Bracken, green or light brown
Carrot (A), green
Choisya (Mexican Orange), parchment
Dock/Sorrel, green or red
Eucalyptus, mole, tinged with blue
Fern, green
Grasses, mixed colours
Holly, dark green or variegated, turning to brown
Hornbeam, dark lime green
Hosta, green
Ivy, dark green or variegated, turning to brown
Lime, lime green
Lonicera, golden brown
Pampas Grass, parchment
Polygonatum (Solomon's Seal), green
Rosmarinus (Rosemary), silver-grey
Senecio (Sea Ragwort), silver
Stachys (Lamb's Tongue), silver

Seedheads

Agapanthus (African Lily), gold
Althaea (Hollyhock), green
Aquilegia (Columbine), green
Bocconia (Plume Poppy), light brown
Clematis, grey or yellow
Digitalis (Foxglove), green
Fennel, green
Gaillardia (Blanket Flower), reddish-brown
Lavatera (Mallow), light brown
Lunaria (Honesty), silver
Montbretia, green
Muscari (Grape Hyacinth), parchment
Nipplewort, brown
Oenothera (Evening Primrose), green
Papaver (Poppy), grey-blue
Phlomis (Jerusalem Sage), grey-green
Salvia (Sage), purple-blue
Scilla (Bluebell), parchment
Sisyrinchium (Satin Flower), green or black
Sweetcorn (A), corn colour
Verbascum, grey or brown

Flowers

GREEN
Amaranthus viridis (A): July–Aug.
Ballota: July
Euphorbia (Spurge): June–July
Helleborus (Hellebore): Jan.–April
Hop: Sept.
Kochia scoparia (Burning Bush) (A): July–Aug.
Moluccella laevis (Bells of Ireland) (A): Aug.–Sept.
Tellima: April–June
Zinnia (A): July onwards

BLUE
Ageratum (Floss Flower) (A): May–Oct.
Caryopteris: Aug.–Sept.
Catananche (Cupid's Dart): June–Sept.
Ceanothus: May–June, Aug.–Sept.
Centaurea (Cornflower) (A): June–Sept.
Delphinium: June–July
Delphinium (Larkspur) (A): June–July
Echinops (Globe Thistle): July–Aug.
Eryngium (Sea Holly): July–Aug.
Galega (Goat's Rue): June–July
Gentiana (Gentian): May–June, July, Sept.
Hydrangea: July–Sept.
Lavandula (Lavender): June–July
Limonium (Statice, Sea Lavender) (A): July–Sept.
Lupinus (Lupin): May–June
Nepeta (Catmint): May–Sept.
Nigella (Love-in-a-Mist) (A): June–Aug.

MAUVE AND PURPLE
Acanthus (Bear's Breeches): July–Aug.
Ageratum (Floss Flower) (A): May–Oct.
Aster (A): Aug.–Sept.
Buddleia (Butterfly Bush): June–Sept.
Centaurea (Cornflower): (A) June–Sept.
Chives: June–July
Clarkia (A): July–Sept.
Dahlia: Aug. onwards
Delphinium: June–July
Globe Artichoke

Helichrysum (Straw Flower) (A): July onwards
Helleborus (Hellebore): Feb.–April
Hydrangea: July–Sept.
Lathyrus (Everlasting Pea): June–Sept.
Liatris (Blazing Star): July–Aug.
Matthiola (Stock) (A): June onwards
Onopordon (Thistle): July–Aug.
Salvia horminum (Clary) (A): June–Sept.
Syringa (Lilac): May–June
Thymus (Thyme): Aug.
Wisteria: May–June
Xeranthemum (A): Aug.–Sept.

RED OR PINK
Ageratum (Floss Flower) (A): May–Oct.
Amaranthus (Love-Lies-Bleeding): July–Oct.
Aster (A): Aug.–Sept.
Astrantia (Masterwort): June–July
Bergenia (Elephant's Ear): Jan–April
Buddleia (Butterfly Bush): June–July
Celosia (A): July–Aug.
Centaurea (Cornflower) (A): June–Sept.
Chrysanthemum ('Fairie'): Aug.
Clarkia (A): July–Sept.
Cytisus (Broom): April–May
Dahlia: Aug. onwards
Delphinium: June–July
Delphinium (Larkspur) (A): June–Aug.
Dianthus (Carnation): flowering dates vary according to species
Geranium: May–Oct.
Heather ('H.E. Beale'): summer
Helichrysum (Straw Flower) (A): July onwards
Hydrangea: July–Sept.
Kochia (Burning Bush) (A): Sept.–Oct.
Lathyrus (Everlasting Pea): June–Sept.
Limonium (Statice, Sea Lavender) (A): July–Sept.
Lupinus (Lupin): May–June
Matthiola (Stock) (A): June onwards
Peonia (Peony): May–June
Polygonum (Knotweed): May–Sept.
Rhodanthe (A): July–Aug.
Rosa (Rose)
Salvia horminum (Clary) (A): June–Sept.
Spiraea: July–Aug.

Syringa (Lilac): May
Tamarix (Tamarisk): Aug.
Xeranthemum (A): Aug.-Sept.
Zinnia (A): July onwards

ORANGE OR GOLD
Calendula (Pot Marigold) (A): May onwards
Dahlia: Aug. onwards
Helichrysum (Straw Flower) (A): July onwards
Physalis (Cape Gooseberry): Aug.-Sept.
Tagetes (African Marigold) (A): Aug. onwards
Zinnia (A): July onwards

YELLOW
Achillea (Yarrow): June-Sept.
Alchemilla (Lady's Mantle): June-Aug.
Allium moly: June-July
Buttercup: May
Calendula (Pot Marigold) (A): May onwards
Celosia (A): July-Aug.
Chrysanthemum: July-Sept.
Cytisus (Broom): April-May
Dahlia (A): Aug. onwards
Helichrysum angustifolium (Curry Plant): July-Aug.
Helichrysum bracteatum (Straw Flower) (A): July onwards
Heliopsis: July-Sept.
Phlomis (Jerusalem Sage): June-July
Rosa (Rose)

WHITE
Achillea ('The Pearl'): June-Aug.
Acroclinium (A): July-Aug.
Ageratum (A) (Floss Flower) (A): May onwards
Allium rosenbachianum: May-June
Allium roseum: June
Ammobium (A): July onwards
Anaphalis (Pearl Everlasting): Aug.-Sept.
Anthemis (Chamomile): June-July
Astrantia (Masterwort): June-July
Centaurea (Cornflower) (A): June-Sept.
Chrysanthemum: July-Sept.
Clarkia (A): July-Sept.
Convallaria (Lily of the Valley): April-May

Cytisus (Broom): April-May
Dahlia: August onwards
Delphinium (Larkspur) (A): June-Aug.
Dianthus (Carnation): flowering dates vary according to species
Gypsophila: June-Aug.
Heather
Helichrysum (A): July onwards
Leek, Onion: June-Aug.
Meadowsweet: June-Aug.
Philadelphus (Mock Orange): June-July
Salvia Horminum (Clary): June-Sept.

Colour Plates

The following dried flowers and leaves are shown in the colour-plate section between pages 32 and 33. References are to Plates 1, 2 and 3.

Achillea 'Moonshine' (Yarrow), 2
Acroclinium, 3
Artemisia, 1
Astilbe, 1

Bergenia, 1

Centaurea (Cornflower), 1, 3
Chrysanthemum 'Wirral Double', 1
Cornflower (*Centaurea*), 1, 3

Dahlia, 1, 2
Delphinium, 1

Echinops (Globe Thistle), 1
Euphorbia robbiae (Spurge), 2

Fern, 2

Globe Thistle (*Echinops*), 1
Golden Rod (*Solidago*), 2

Helichrysum bracteatum (Straw Flower), 2, 3
Heliopsis, 2
Hosta leaf, 2

Lamb's Tongue (*Stachys lanata*), 1
Larkspur, 1, 3
Limonium (Sea Lavender, Statice), 2, 3
Love-in-a-Mist (*Nigella*), 3

Marigold, 3
Meadow Rue (*Thalictrum*), 2, 3

Nigella seedheads (Love-in-a-Mist), 3

Peony, 1, 2
Polygonum Bistorta (Snakeweed), 1, 3
Poppy seedheads, 1

Rose, 1, 2, 3

Santolina (Cotton Lavender), 2
Scabious leaf, 1
Sea Lavender (*Limonium*), 2, 3
Sea Ragwort (*Senecio maritima*), 1
Senecio maritima (Sea Ragwort), 1
Snakeweed (*Polygonum Bistorta*), 1, 3
Solidago (Golden Rod), 2
Spurge (*Euphorbia robbiae*), 2
Stachys lanata (Lamb's Tongue), 1
Statice (*Limonium*), 2, 3
Straw Flower (*Helichrysum bracteatum*), 2, 3

Thalictrum leaf (Meadow Rue), 2, 3

Yarrow (*Achillea*), 2

Zinnia, 1, 2, 3

Some Botanical Terms

Annual: a plant that blooms only in the year of seeding and then dies.

Biennial: a plant that lives for two years, usually flowering the year after the seed is sown.

Bract: a small leaf growing below the calyx.

Calyx: leaves forming the outer case of a bud.

Deciduous: a shrub or tree that sheds its leaves annually.

Evergreen: a shrub or tree that keeps its leaves throughout the year.

Floret: a small individual flower, in a mass making up a complete bloom.

Genus: a group of flowers which contains several species having the same structural characteristics.

Glaucous: covered with a dull bluish-green 'bloom'.

Leaflet: a small leaf of a compound leaf.

Palmate: palm-shaped.

Panicle: a loose cluster of flowers.

Perennial: flowering for many seasons.

Pinnate: a series of leaflets on each side of a leaf stalk.

Raceme: a cluster of flowers, each flower being attached to the main stem by a small stalk.

Species: a group of plants between which there are only minor differences.

Umbel: a cluster of flowers on stalks of nearly equal length issuing from a central point.

Whorl: leaves or flowers encircling a stem.